The Ostrich and The EMU

Policy Choices Facing the UK

Panel Members

Rupert Pennant-Rea *Chairman, Caspian Securities Limited*
Chairman

Professor David Miles
Imperial College, University of London, and Merrill Lynch
Rapporteur

Professor Charles Bean
London School of Economics and Political Science and CEPR

Professor David Begg
Birkbeck College, University of London, and CEPR

Sir Peter Gregson KCB
Director, Scottish Power plc and former Permanent Secretary, Department of Trade and Industry

Jeremy Hardie
Chairman, W H Smith Group plc

Sir Tim Lankester
Director, School of Oriental and African Studies, University of London

Professor Richard Portes
London Business School and CEPR

Dr Ann Robinson
Director General, National Association of Pension Funds

Dr Paul Seabright
Churchill College, University of Cambridge, and CEPR

Martin Wolf
Associate Editor, Financial Times

The Ostrich and The EMU

Policy Choices Facing the UK

Report of an Independent Panel Chaired by Rupert Pennant-Rea

Centre for Economic Policy Research

The Centre for Economic Policy Research is a network of over 350 Research Fellows, based primarily in European universities. The Centre coordinates its Fellows' research activities and communicates their results to the public and private sectors. CEPR is an entrepreneur, developing research initiatives with the producers, consumers and sponsors of research. Established in 1983, CEPR is a European economics research organization with uniquely wide-ranging scope and activities.

CEPR is a registered educational charity. Institutional (core) finance for the Centre is provided by major grants from the Economic and Social Research Council, under which an ESRC Resource Centre operates within CEPR; the Esmée Fairbairn Charitable Trust; the Bank of England; the European Monetary Institute and the Bank for International Settlements; 20 national central banks and 40 companies. None of these organizations gives prior review to the Centre's publications, nor do they necessarily endorse the views expressed therein.

The Centre is pluralist and non-partisan, bringing economic research to bear on the analysis of medium- and long-run policy questions. CEPR research may include views on policy, but the Executive Committee of the Centre does not give prior review to its publications, and the Centre takes no institutional policy positions. The opinions expressed in this report are those of the authors and not those of the Centre for Economic Policy Research.

9 May 1997

25–28 Old Burlington Street, London W1X 1LB, UK
Tel: (44 171) 878 2900
Fax: (44 171) 878 2999
Email: cepr@cepr.org

British Library Cataloguing in Publication Data
A Catalogue record for this book is available from the British Library

ISBN 1 898128 31 6

Printed in Great Britain by Short Run Press, Exeter

Contents

List of Figures

List of Tables

Foreword

A year ago, in discussions with politicians on both sides of the 'to join or not to join' debate on EMU, we identified a major gap in public discussion: what the policy-makers would have to do, in or out, how quickly they would have to make these decisions, and how this would affect the timing of entry should we go in. The run-up to the general election generated increasing heat on the desirability of joining a monetary union, less light on the substantive issues, and virtually nothing to fill the gap facing policy-makers of whatever leaning. I believe this Report does the job by setting out a framework both for discussion by the informed public and for detailed implementation by the policy machine, in the light of whatever political decisions are taken about entry.

The Esmée Fairbairn Charitable Trust supported the work of the Panel and this publication, and we are most grateful to the Trustees and the Director, not least for their advice in initial discussions of how the Panel should proceed. The Trust had previously commissioned the November 1993 CEPR Report, *Independent and Accountable: A New Mandate for the Bank of England* (for which the Panel was chaired by Lord Roll). Subsequent events – from the decision in early 1994 to publish the minutes of the meetings of Chancellor and Governor to the announcement by the new Labour government of a framework for the Bank's independence – have, we believe, both benefited from and justified that Panel's deliberations. I am confident that this Report will have an equal impact.

As a member of the Panel myself, I can testify to the outstanding contribution of Rupert Pennant-Rea as its Chairman and his work, together with our excellent rapporteur, David Miles, in writing up its conclusions. We all appreciate greatly the efforts of CEPR staff in assisting the Panel, especially Kate Millward, CEPR's Publications Manager, who has produced the publication so quickly.

RICHARD PORTES

12 May 1997

Preface

When CEPR first asked me to chair this study group, I groaned. Surely everything that could be said on EMU had already been said, at least a dozen times? In fact, that isn't true. For several years the UK debate has been artificially restricted to those subjects that would not cause the main political parties to fracture completely. As a result, the practical issues have largely been neglected.

This report is about practicalities. At the first meeting of our study group, I asked all the members to avoid theology; ideally, I said, none of us would reveal a particular view on whether the UK should or shouldn't join EMU. Even now, I don't know what most of them think about that big question. For their restraint, and much else, I thank them. I also want to single out Professor David Miles, a rapporteur of great skill and patience.

The surest conclusion to emerge from this report is that, 'in' or 'out', the UK will be affected by EMU, and its policy machine must react. Doing nothing is not an option. It may be many years before the consequences of going in or staying out become clear; but even during the next few months, there will be plans and decisions to make which will greatly affect the UK's long-term economic interests – 'in' or 'out'.

RUPERT PENNANT-REA

9 May 1997

Executive Summary

This report analyses the policy implications for the United Kingdom of the single European currency.

Whatever decision the government eventually takes, there will be big changes in the economic environment, and these changes require policy responses. Some are widely recognized: for example, a decision to join EMU would require that the Bank of England have more than operational independence over monetary policy. Other implications of joining, however, have not been analysed so carefully. For instance, being in a monetary union would be less problematic for the UK if its sensitivity to interest rates were more like that of other EMU members. Could that be engineered and, if so, how? Any such policies would take time to implement and bear fruit, which therefore affects the date when it would be sensible to join EMU.

The UK government has four possible strategies for EMU:

1. Join at the start.
2. Decide to join, but do so later.
3. Wait and see. The pragmatic agnostic's position: if EMU works, then join at some unspecified date.
4. Decide in principle not to join.

Joining at the start would require:

■ A fully independent central bank by the end of 1998. The government would therefore have to attach high priority to drafting and passing a new Bank of England Act that was in important respects different from that outlined by the Chancellor when, on 6 May 1997, he announced his plans to give the Bank operational independence.

- A significant tightening in macroeconomic policy before the UK was subject to an interest rate that would probably be much lower than it needs for its current cyclical state. Interest rates in EMU's first-wave candidates are now 3% below UK rates, and the gap might be wider in a year's time.

- A lower exchange rate.

- Enhancing automatic fiscal stabilizers, to compensate for the loss of autonomy over monetary policy.

- Reducing the tax incentive to use debt. This will help make the transmission mechanism of monetary policy in the UK more like that in other EMU candidates.

A decision to *delay entry* by, say, three or four years would ease or eliminate the practical problems of trying to achieve these things in time for the start of EMU. It will not be imperative to make the Bank of England fully independent by the end of 1998, though legislation should not be delayed for long. It will also be desirable to bring in legislative measures to enhance the fiscal stabilizers; they will then have a chance to start working.

But the bigger advantages of delay relate to conjunctural and exchange rate concerns. By 2001 or 2002 the EMU interest rate may well be broadly what the UK economy needs in the cyclical circumstances it will then find itself.

A *wait and see strategy* has the obvious advantage that some of the uncertainty about EMU (on the operation of monetary policy, on the demand for and value of the Euro, on the strains generated by a single short term interest rate for all the 'ins') will be reduced. But in order to keep open the option of joining EMU some way down the road it would still be desirable to reduce the fiscal deficit and remove tax incentives to use debt. It might also be sensible to draft the amendments to the Bank of England Act (required under the government's plans to grant it operational independence) in a way which allowed it to operate as part of the European System of Central Banks should the UK join EMU.

If the UK were to *stay out of a monetary union* how the value of sterling fluctuated against the Euro would be of great significance. The sterling-Euro exchange rate would be much more important for UK business than any bilateral rate now is. Sharp fluctuations in the rate would be more damaging than a similar fluctuation in a bilateral rate today. And because countries inside the single currency area could not independently do much to alter their competitiveness against the UK they are likely to be more sensitive to the exchange rate implications of UK policy.

The surest way for the UK to minimize discrimination against UK-based firms is to participate actively in the development of the Single Market. If the UK stays out of EMU, this participation will be even more important (and perhaps more difficult too). Much will depend on attitude. If the UK is seen as a constructive agnostic on EMU, it will be listened to on subjects such as competition policy. If it comes across as a whingeing outsider, it won't.

1

Introduction

This report analyses the policy implications for the United Kingdom of the single European currency. It does not judge whether the UK should or should not join EMU; rather it emphasizes that whatever decision the government eventually takes, there will be big changes in the economic environment, and these changes require policy responses. Some are widely recognized: for example, a decision to join EMU would require that the Bank of England have more than operational independence over monetary policy; the Bank's objectives (the inflation target) could not be changed by the government nor could there be an override which, even temporarily, let government give instructions on interest rates. But other implications of joining have not been analysed so carefully. For instance, being in a monetary union would be less problematic for the UK if its sensitivity to interest rates were more like that of other EMU members. Could that be engineered and, if so, how? Any such policies would take time to implement and bear fruit, which therefore affects the date when it would be sensible to join EMU.

Whatever decision the government eventually takes, there will be big changes in the economic environment, and these changes require policy responses.

In the same way, staying outside EMU would have policy implications that have not been properly considered. Because the Euro would be much more important for the UK than any existing bilateral exchange rate, it would prompt UK financial institutions to alter their portfolios. It would also heighten the sensitivity of overseas holdings of UK financial assets to perceived policy differences between the UK and the Continent. All this would have implications for macroeconomic policy.

The key message of this report is that time lags are crucial. It takes time to change tax rates, or to change the Bank of England's status, or to increase the role of fiscal stabilisers or to move into fiscal surplus. It takes even longer for the impact of changes in taxes or regulations to feed through. Without a clear idea of the time lags involved, it is hard to set priorities and make decisions on entry.

The key message of this report is that time lags are crucial. Without a clear idea of the time lags involved, it is hard to set priorities and make decisions on entry.

The report does not deal directly with those issues that vitally concern business but not the policy machine. Although we recognize their importance (how should UK banks react to the uncertainties surrounding a single currency? what will be the cost to retailers of switching to a new currency?) they are better handled by others. Instead, the report concentrates on those consequences of EMU that can be influenced by government. Even then, because public policy can affect companies and individuals in so many ways, the report has to cover a wide range of issues.

Our aim is twofold:

■ to analyse the changes in microeconomic and macroeconomic policies that will make a single currency work better if the UK does join EMU;

■ to investigate how polices might need to change so as to reduce any costs, and increase any benefits, of *not* joining.

What we do not do is draw up a full balance sheet of benefits and costs of joining or not joining; accordingly, we make no attempt to judge whether the UK should join. In many areas, policies will need to change more if the UK joins EMU than if it stays outside. Given our aims, we naturally concentrate on such changes. But it would be wrong to interpret this to mean that adopting a single currency is more costly or problematic than remaining outside. That conclusion could be reached only by also looking at the potential benefits of joining EMU and the possible costs of remaining outside.

The Report is divided into three sections. Chapter 2 focuses on setting policy instruments after EMU has been formed: in macro-economic terms, the overall stance of fiscal policy, funding strategy and labour market issues; and for microeconomic policy, those issues connected with tax rates, competition and regional policy. Chapter 3 covers the institutional setting of policy, and particularly those issues connected with the Bank of England and the framework for monetary policy and financial supervision. Chapter 4 highlights the timing and transitional issues involved in going in or staying out. In Chapter 5 we summarize the report and offer a simple matrix of the options and the implications.

2

Setting the policy levers

2.1 | Issues as an 'in'

Any country that joins EMU will lose the power to set
national interest rates and change its exchange rate
against other 'ins'. Inside EMU, the UK would have to accept
the same short-term interest rate as the rest of Europe; and
longer-term interest rates would differ from those in other
countries by risk premia that are not easily influenced by policy.
The significance of this change depends on several factors: the
size of economic shocks that are specific to the UK; the degree of
flexibility in labour markets; and differences in the way that a
common European monetary policy would affect EMU members.

Clearly, the UK's economic cycle has recently been out of line
with the cycle on the Continent. This partly reflects differences
in monetary policy, and to that extent joining EMU would make
the UK cycle more like that of other members. But even EMU
would not eliminate some distinguishing features of the UK
economy. As a result, the effect of certain kinds of shocks (e.g. oil
price changes, cyclical movements in North America and Asia)
and of a particular European monetary policy may remain
significantly different for the UK compared with the EMU
average.

The obvious structural differences include:

- **Oil production**: The UK is a sizeable net exporter of oil,
  and the only EU country that is a net exporter of all
  primary energy (see Figures 2.1 and 2.2). This will continue
  for some time: last year the Department of Trade and
  Industry estimated that the UK's remaining reserves of oil

Any country that joins EMU will lose the power to set national interest rates and change its exchange rate against other 'ins'. The significance of this change depends on several factors.

3

and gas were between twice and six times greater than total production since 1980.

■ **Personal debt**: The UK's stock of household debt is, and is likely to remain, substantially higher than the EU average (see Table 2.1). Much of that debt is at variable rates of interest, which means the transmission mechanism of monetary policy works differently in the UK.

■ **Company borrowing**: Corporate use of the bond market (often at fixed rates of interest) is relatively low in the UK, and reliance on short-term bank loans has been above the EU average (see Table 2.2).

■ **Public expenditure**: As a proportion of GDP, government expenditure and taxes are lower in the UK than in most EU countries (see Figure 2.3).

■ **Trade**: The proportion of UK trade that is currently with other EU members is below average (see Figure 2.4).

Of course, most countries are unusual in some respects. It is possible to think up criteria that make Germany an outlier, or that put France at one extreme or the other on a table or chart. It is, therefore, helpful to have some wider measure of how far countries are subject to idiosyncratic demand and supply shocks. One simple guide is the correlation of national GDP growth with growth in the EU as a whole. On this measure, the UK, along with Finland and Ireland, is indeed in the group of economies that have not been highly correlated with the EU cycle (see Table 2.3).

It is possible, however, that cycles would become more synchronized as a result of EMU, because monetary policy would be common. If changes in national interest rates had in the past been a source of idiosyncratic demand shocks (rather than a dampening influence), then cycles would become more closely aligned. So it is useful to separate out the demand and supply shocks, and gauge how correlated they have been.

It is possible that cycles would become more synchronized as a result of EMU, because monetary policy would be common.

Some studies have used sophisticated econometric techniques to try to establish the pattern: Figure 2.5 shows the correlations estimated by Bayoumi and Eichengreen (1996), based on data from 1960 to 1993[1]. They found that the UK had a relatively low correlation of both demand and supply shocks, though Finland and Ireland were even more out of line with the EU norm.

Any such conclusions are based on the past. The more important question is whether the idiosyncrasies of the UK

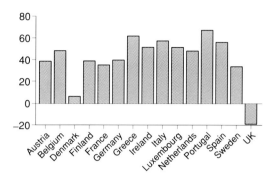

Figure 2.1 1995 Imports of crude oil & petroleum (% of domestic energy consumption)

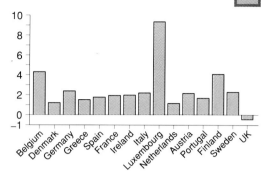

Figure 2.2 1995 Net imports of primary energy (Tonnes of oil equivalent per person)

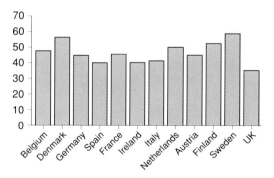

Figure 2.3 Total tax receipts of general government (% of GDP in 1994)

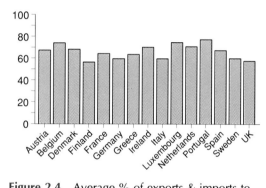

Figure 2.4 Average % of exports & imports to EC in 1995 (% of total)

(*Source: Eurostat Yearbook* (1996), Office of Official Publications of the EC, Luxembourg)

Table 2.1 Financial liabilities of the household sector (% of GDP)

UK	79	(1995)
Norway	70	(1993)
Spain	58	(1995)
Germany	56	(1995)
Sweden	54	(1994)
France	50	(1995)
Finland	41	(1994)
Italy	24	(1995)

Source: OECD balance sheets of non-financial sector

Table 2.2 Corporate bonds outstanding in 1995 (% of GDP)

Sweden	69.5
Germany	61.2
Belgium	55.5
Austria	36.5
Switzerland	35.8
Norway	19.2
Finland	19.2
Italy	13.7
France	11.6
Iceland	9.6
Netherlands	7.6
Spain	6.1
Ireland	3.2
UK	**2.9**

Source: Merrill Lynch 'The Size & Structure of World Bond Markets', October 1996

Table 2.3 Correlation of the annual growth of National GDP with EU GDP, 1961–93

France	0.91
Belgium	0.87
Germany	0.85
Italy	0.79
Spain	0.79
Austria	0.78
Portugal	0.76
Netherlands	0.75
Denmark	0.69
Sweden	0.67
Greece	0.66
Luxembourg	0.64
UK	**0.63**
Finland	0.59
Ireland	0.20

economy will persist into the future, especially if the UK joined EMU. One of the likely benefits of monetary union would be increased trade and integration, which would affect the structure of economies (probably making them more synchronized). But even that is not certain. It is conceivable that the lower costs of cross-border trade would encourage more specialization, so that individual EMU members became more dependent on certain industries and therefore more susceptible to particular industrial shocks. Recent empirical work by Frankel and Rose (1996) suggests that more trade between countries does, on balance, increase the correlation of business cycle activity; but even if economic shocks were uniform across the single currency area, their effects could vary. The impact of interest rates and the flexibility of labour markets can and do differ between countries,

Figure 2.5 Correlations of the demand and supply shocks with Germany (*Source:* Bayoumi and Eichengreen (1996))

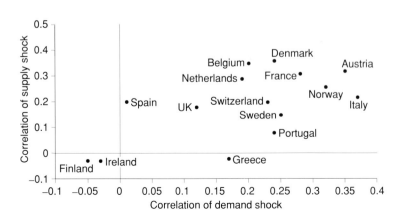

which means that a common monetary policy will, from time to time, be unsuitable for certain regions.

In short, the UK is different, but not uniquely so. Its economic conditions, and the monetary policy that is best suited to deal with them, will sometimes deviate significantly from the EMU average. Indeed, all EU members will find that a common monetary policy is sometimes less than ideal (either too tight or too loose). Of course economic conditions can differ substantially even *within* the UK, and in theory this causes strains for a common UK monetary policy; but labour mobility and the scale of fiscal transfers between regions are much greater within the UK than will ever be the case within a European single currency area.

The analysis thus far has major implications for fiscal policy, the labour market, and regional and competition policy. We consider the fiscal issues first.

2.1.1 Fiscal policy

When a country loses autonomy over monetary policy, any counter-cyclical efforts have to rely on fiscal policy. In the UK, by contrast, over the past two decades monetary policy has increasingly been used to control aggregate demand, while tax and spending decisions have become part of a longer-term framework. If these fiscal variables had to play more of a counter-cyclical role, how should that be done?

When a country loses autonomy over monetary policy, fiscal policy needs to play a greater counter-cyclical role.

In particular:

- Do the tools of fiscal policy need to become more flexible?

- Is it better to enhance fiscal stabilisers (so that the direct impact of fiscal policy on demand is *automatically* increased by more in a downswing and reduced by more in an upswing) or to increase discretion over fiscal policy (i.e. make fine tuning easier)?

- Would EMU membership involve limits on the size of the budget deficit (specified in some form of stability pact) that require substantial changes to the UK's fiscal stance?

- How will the effects of an active fiscal policy differ from those of an active monetary policy?

One way to think about these issues is to ask how changes in fiscal policy could mimic the effect of shifts in domestic interest rates designed to cool down or revive the economy. Changes in interest rates have had substantial effects upon the exchange rate, with consequent effects on short-term competitiveness. They have also affected the spending of households and companies, the precise amount depending partly on the value and distribution of debt. If the option of increasing interest rates in the UK is not available, at least some of the same effects might be achieved by reducing the tax deductibility of interest payments (and raising it when a looser monetary policy is needed). Unfortunately, this approach would require frequent changes in *de facto* tax rates, which is difficult and undesirable.

In contrast, sales taxes (VAT and excise duties) can be changed quite quickly, and will swiftly reduce or boost tax revenues. To the extent that these changes affect the timing of spending, they do so in a helpful way. If macroeconomic policy needs to be tightened, a temporary increase in sales tax may persuade consumers to postpone spending. This approach has one major weakness: in an overheating economy, raising indirect tax rates adds to inflationary pressures at just the wrong time.

On the expenditure side, there is even less scope for fiscal flexibility. It is not desirable (nor politically feasible) to reverse decisions on big items of government expenditure at short notice. It is less costly to change the timing of spending programmes that have already been agreed, but even this has drawbacks.

Beyond these traditional forms of fiscal flexibility, there are other possible measures that could be considered. One is contingent tax refunds: if GDP falls, for example, taxpayers receive lump sum rebates. Conceptually, these would be similar to cold weather payments to pensioners. However, the lump-sum nature of payments means that their impact on the distribution of income will be regressive and is not attractive; and no government would like to announce a lump-sum levy if policy had to be tightened.

Perhaps the least-bad method would be to allow taxpayers to hold back some of their (income) tax bill in a downswing, and then pay that extra element back in an upswing. This would change the timing of tax receipts, but not their overall value over the cycle. Such a scheme also has a distributional advantage: it would favour small businesses and households with the least access to credit. Even then it is questionable whether the impact on consumption will be great, because people may save most of any temporary rebates so as to smooth their own spending over the cycle.

To run through these options is to highlight their inherent difficulties. There are no simple and non-distortionary ways of boosting fiscal flexibility to offset the loss of monetary autonomy. The most that a government can aim for is a full role for the automatic fiscal stabilisers, so that surpluses would fall (or deficits rise) in a downswing that was unusually sharp in the UK. One element of this strategy is that spending plans for projects that are not cyclically sensitive should be set in a long-term context and *not* adjusted through the cycle. A second requirement is that all cyclically sensitive spending (e.g. total expenditure on unemployment benefits) be allowed to fluctuate freely with no attempt to cut such expenditure because the deficit is rising sharply. *Provided that the cyclically adjusted fiscal position is sustainable*, sharp movements in the fiscal deficit through the cycle should not be a cause for concern. A policy of focusing on the cyclically adjusted fiscal balance, allowing the deficit or surplus to fluctuate sharply from year to year and even increasing cyclical variability by introducing flexibility in the timing of tax payments is what we mean by enhancing the automatic fiscal stabilisers. Inside EMU, however, will it be possible to let these stabilisers work so that fiscal policy can be eased significantly in a downturn? This depends on how the rules on excessive deficits will operate.

There are no simple and non-distortionary ways of boosting fiscal flexibility to offset the loss of monetary autonomy.

2.1.2 Rules on deficits

At the EU Dublin summit in December 1996, governments agreed on penalties for running excessive deficits. Under the Stability and Growth Pact, any EMU member whose deficit exceeds 3% of GDP will be reported to the EU's committee of Finance Ministers, ECOFIN. The committee will then have to decide whether there are exceptional circumstances that would justify waiving the penalties. The offending country would not be fined if its GDP had fallen by 2% or more over a year. For falls in GDP of between 0.75% and 2%, ECOFIN would have discretion over the level of fines. Otherwise, save in other (undefined) exceptional circumstances, there would be a fine of 0.2% of GDP for exceeding the 3% limit, plus an additional 0.1% for each 1% over the 3% ceiling, up to a maximum of 0.5% of GDP.

It is hard to know whether these rules will be applied in practice, and there must be some doubt about how effective a sanction they would be. But in principle, fines could be very big. In 1993 the UK's budget deficit was just under 7% of GDP, while

In the longer term a strategy of, on average, running a tight policy (e.g. aiming for a small surplus) could be sensible.

its GDP rose by 2.2%. Strictly applied, the rules agreed at Dublin would have meant a fine for the UK of about £3 billion (the maximum 0.5% of GDP). Over the whole period 1992–96, the cumulative fines would have been about £15 billion (2.3% of annual GDP), and ECOFIN would have had no automatic discretion to waive or reduce them.

Assuming that the Pact really will be applied, it has one major implication for the design of counter-cyclical policy. In the longer term a strategy of, on average, running a tight policy (e.g. aiming for a small surplus) could be sensible. In a downturn, such an approach would then give greater scope for loosening policy without hitting the 3% limit. Though this sounds perfectly rational, it presents a huge challenge for the government. Over the past thirty years (when interest rates played a big role in counter-cyclical policy) the average deficit was a little over 3% of GDP and the standard deviation of the deficit to GDP ratio in the UK was about 2.9% (see Figure 2.6). The deficit was less than 3% of GDP in fewer than half of the years. Assuming (a) the same standard deviation in the future and (b) only a 10% chance of the deficit going above 3% of GDP, fiscal policy would normally need to be set so as to generate a surplus of about 1% of GDP_2. To get there from where the UK currently is would require a substantial tightening of policy: cuts in spending and increases in tax of the order of 4% of GDP (over £25 billion).

This calculation is based on a period when UK inflation was high and variable, which tends to make the inflation unadjusted deficit (the focus of the Pact) more volatile and higher. If inflation were to be lower and less variable, then unadjusted deficits would almost certainly be lower and less variable as well.

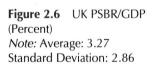

Figure 2.6 UK PSBR/GDP (Percent)
Note: Average: 3.27
Standard Deviation: 2.86

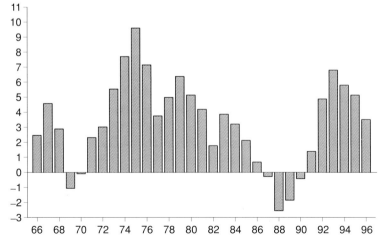

The variability in the ratio of the primary balance (excluding debt interest) to GDP, which is less affected by changes in inflation, is indeed a bit lower than the variability in the overall deficit; but the difference is quite small. Against this, the UK's fiscal record comes from a period when monetary policy itself was being actively used to minimize shifts in the budgetary position. It is, therefore, hard to prescribe exactly the cyclically adjusted fiscal balance in EMU; but without doubt the average stance of policy needs to be much tighter than in the recent past, so as to allow fiscal flexibility without hitting the 3% limit.

That is a powerful conclusion, but it is by no means the end of the fiscal story. The next section deals with other budgetary issues that are in their own way just as significant.

2.1.3 Fiscal autonomy in EMU

There are two categories of questions connected with fiscal autonomy, one macro and the other micro:

1. Would EMU membership affect the scope for running deficits and surpluses?

2. Will national governments be free to set specific tax rates and allowances that are different from those of other EMU members?

The first issue goes well beyond the Growth and Stability Pact, important though that is. A key issue is whether, as an 'in', a national government's ability to raise revenue to finance national spending will be reduced. There are several ways that could happen. Most fundamental would be a big increase in labour mobility, since that would erode government's ability to raise revenue and redistribute spending. If people can easily move to countries where taxes are low, then some of the better off may opt out of a redistributive tax and spending system to which they are net contributors. In the extreme case redistributive policies could be organized only on a centralized, EU-wide basis. In principle, labour mobility is likely to be enhanced by EMU; in practice, the effect is unlikely to be great. Non-currency factors (language and cultural differences) probably have much more influence on migration, and these are not likely to change as a result of EMU.

In fact, the pressures for more centralization of spending are likely to stem from labour *immobility*. This could arise if some countries have high and rising unemployment, and want greater fiscal transfers from the EU. If the transfers were even roughly as

A key issue is whether, as an 'in', a national government's ability to raise revenue to finance national spending will be reduced.

large as those within existing currency areas (the US, the UK, Germany, France, Italy) the EU central budget would need to increase substantially as a proportion of aggregate GDP.

Is there a case for such a rise? Where unemployment is high, or has recently risen, some members may indeed want more fiscal transfers. But the case for *permanent* transfers to countries with higher than average unemployment is not strong. Giving up the right to devalue and set national interest rates may well mean that the level of EU-wide interest rates is wrong for some economies from time to time; but because these periods of unsuitable monetary policy and their effects are not permanent, the fiscal transfers should be only temporary.

The same point can be made in another way. As history shows, the option to devalue or to run a looser monetary policy does not generate permanently lower unemployment. It follows that the cost of giving up such options is unlikely to be permanently higher unemployment. Unemployment rates may differ persistently within EMU (just as they do now); but the causes, and remedies, are much more likely to be microeconomic than macroeceonomic. So permanent fiscal transfers are the wrong policy response. (See von Hagen and Hammond (1995).)

A similar argument applies to the question of pooling national spending and revenues. Recent OECD estimates show that the scale of unfunded future pension liabilities is much higher for most Continental countries than for the UK (see Roseveare et al. (1996)). In a currency union it is neither necessary nor desirable that the revenues for funding these (or any other components of national spending) are centralized. Nor are there any plans that this should occur; and the statutes of the European Central Bank (ECB) explicitly rule out any use of its resources for financing national deficits.

None of this guarantees that the central EU budget will remain small. Even a much bigger EU budget is, however, unlikely to constrain national fiscal flexibility because, in macroeconomic terms, what matters is the ability to affect *at the margin* the balance between domestic revenue and domestic spending.

The second point about fiscal autonomy is a micro one: the freedom of governments to have their own tax and benefits system. There is no necessary link between adopting a single currency and changing a national system of taxes and benefits. The Maastricht Treaty has no direct implications for the harmonization of tax structures and welfare programmes. But a single currency would probably affect the substitutability of goods,

Even a much bigger EU budget is unlikely to constrain national fiscal flexibility, because in macroeconomic terms what matters is the ability to affect at the margin.

services and financial assets. The mobility of capital (and, to a smaller extent, labour) is also likely to be affected. We consider the microeconomic area under four headings: indirect taxes; income taxes and benefits; taxes on companies; and capital taxes.

Indirect taxes

The EU's current approach to value added taxation does place restrictions on the VAT rates that EU governments may set. The standard rate cannot be under 15% and no more than two reduced rates are allowed on a specified list of goods and services. Certain goods taxed at below 5% in 1991 may continue to be taxed at those rates.

Despite these restrictions, VAT rates still vary widely across the EU (see Table 2.4), and neither rates nor exemptions have converged much over the past ten years.

Similarly, the share of indirect taxes in total tax revenue also varies considerably from country to country, though not as

Table 2.4 VAT rates (%) in the EU, at 1 July 1996

	Standard	Reduced[a]	Higher
Austria	20	10, 12	–
Belgium	21	1, 6, 12	–
Denmark	25	–	–
Finland	22	12, 17	–
Germany	15	7	–
Spain	16	4, 7	–
France	20.6	2.1, 5.5	–
Greece	18	4.8	–
Ireland	21	2.8, 12.5	–
Italy	19	4, 10, 16	–
Luxembourg	15	3, 6, 12	–
Netherlands	17.5	6	–
Portugal[c]	17 (13)	5, 12, (4, 8)	30
Sweden	25	6, 12	–
UK[b]	17.5	0, 8	–

Note: Lower rates apply in the autonomous regions of Portugal.

[a] The Rates Directive (92/77/EEC) allows member states to have a maximum of two reduced rates, one of which may be below 5% provided that either (i) it was in force on 1 January 1991 or (ii) the standard rate was 13% or below at that time. It also allows member states to have an intermediate rate between 12% and the standard rate.

[b] Zero rate applies to a wide variety of goods and services. Reduced rate of 5% applies to hotel accommodation in the Isle of Man.

[c] Rates in brackets apply in the autonomous regions of Madeira and the Azores archipelagos.

Source: HM Customs & Excise Annual Report, 1996, Table C.8

The current rules set lower limits on VAT rates leaving scope for variations in sales taxes to act as a fiscal stabiliser.

much as that of employers' and employees' social security contributions (see Table 2.5). Furthermore, the current rules set lower limits on VAT rates leaving scope for variations in sales taxes to act as a fiscal stabiliser.

Would EMU require rapid and complete harmonization of indirect taxes? The experience of the United States suggests not. There, individual states have rates of sales tax that vary as much as in EU countries. It seems that non-currency factors ensure that such differences persist. For example, the only land border that the UK shares with another potential EMU member is with Ireland. The transport costs of cross-border shopping will, therefore, remain significant for the vast majority of Britons, and the overall costs of cross-border shopping may not fall much if the UK shares a common currency. Even today, someone crossing the Channel to shop in northern France has virtually no currency risk (since all transactions are done at the exchange rate for that day). The only difference is the cost of currency conversion, which would disappear if the UK and France adopt the Euro. This cost is not trivial, but it is surely not large enough to require that, inside EMU, the UK would have to adopt a common system of indirect tax to avoid massive tax arbitrage.

For other EU members, though, tax-driven, cross-border shopping is more important, and will probably increase when a single currency is introduced. The European Commission has recently published proposals for much greater harmonization of VAT systems within the EU (including equalization of the VAT rate). For example, it says that, for VAT purposes, companies should have one location (see European Commission (1996)). If such proposals were adopted, the UK would have to raise its standard rate of VAT and remove zero-rating of certain items. It is worth noting, however, that decisions on VAT changes are currently subject to the unanimous approval of member states. Anyway, the introduction of a more harmonized scheme of indirect taxation is not formally linked to the prospect of a single currency. It would, however, certainly reduce the contribution that variations in indirect tax could make to counter-cyclical policy.

Income taxes and benefits

In or out of EMU, countries are less likely to harmonize their income taxes and welfare systems than their indirect taxes. Mobility of labour within Europe is low (perhaps particularly among the British) and people are unlikely to migrate in large numbers for tax reasons alone. The same goes for welfare payments and public services (state pensions, unemployment benefits, sickness benefits, state medical and education provision) which already vary widely across the EU, and have not prompted much migration. It is not obvious that any of this inertia would change simply because the Euro came into existence.

In or out of EMU, countries are less likely to harmonize their income taxes and welfare systems than their indirect taxes.

Taxes on companies

Although European citizens may remain relatively immobile, European companies probably will not. Once currency risk is eliminated, companies will pay more attention to differences in the costs of doing business in different countries. As an 'in', the UK (with relatively low employment taxes and corporation taxes (see Table 2.5 on p. 16)) would become more attractive for businesses wishing to sell in Europe. Precisely for that reason, other EMU members may try to harmonize company taxes. The Ruding Committee has already proposed maximum and minimum corporate tax rates in the EU, and a common basis for calculating taxable profit (see European Commission (1992)).

Pressure to harmonize corporate tax would probably be just as strong if the UK opts out of EMU. If its corporate-tax system were thought to be attracting companies from the Continent, EMU members would probably complain that the UK was making the whole project more difficult. They might then feel justified in discriminating against the UK in other areas (procurement policy, etc.) 'for the greater European good'.

Capital taxes

If companies are more footloose than people, financial capital is positively nomadic. With currency risk removed, all Euro-denominated assets will become closer substitutes for one another, no matter where they are issued. The implication of this is that, for investors facing a particular set of tax rules, the expected post-tax returns on assets (e.g., government bonds issued by 'ins') should be closer than is now the case, when currency risk still matters. It is not clear, however, that national rules on capital taxes therefore need to be closer. Currently, double tax agreements mean that holdings of many classes of foreign assets are taxed as if they were domestic assets[3], so

Table 2.5 Taxes in the Community in 1994 (% of GDP)

	Current taxes on income and wealth	Taxes linked to production and imports excl. VAT	VAT on products	Capital taxes	Employers' actual social contributions	Employees' actual social contributions	Social contributions by non-employed	Taxes and social contributions
Belgium	17.9	5.2	6.6	0.3	9.4	5.2	1.2	45.7
Denmark	31.4	7.8	9.4	0.2	0.3	1.3	0.0	50.5
Germany	11.1	6.0	6.4	0.1	8.1	7.1	3.0	41.7
Greece	(a)5.2	(a)6.9	(a)6.6	(a)0.3	(a)4.7	(a)3.9	–	–
Spain	(b)12.0	(b)4.9	(b)4.7	(b)0.2	(b)9.2	(b)2.2	(b)1.9	(b)35.0
France	9.5	7.4	6.7	0.6	11.8	5.9	1.5	43.4
Ireland	16.1	8.1	6.8	0.2	3.2	2.3	0.3	36.9
Italy	15.0	6.6	5.1	0.1	8.8	2.8	1.6	40.0
Luxembourg	14.2	10.2	5.5	0.1	5.7	4.8	1.7	42.4
Netherlands	14.1	5.6	6.2	0.3	3.2	12.5	3.9	45.8
Austria	11.3	7.9	8.3	0.1	7.2	6.6	1.2	42.7
Portugal	(c)10.2	(c)7.8	(c)6.4	(c)0.1	(c)6.7	(c)3.5	(c)0.3	(c)35.2
Finland	(b)16.0	(b)14.8	(b)0.0	(b)0.2	(b)10.3	(b)2.7	(b)1.6	(b)45.5
Sweden	21.5	6.9	8.2	0.1	12.6	0.9	0.3	50.4
UK	12.6	7.1	6.2	0.2	3.5	2.9	0.2	32.8

Note: (a) = 1989   (b) = 1993   (c) = 1992
Source: Eurostat: 'Taxes and Social Contributions 1983–94', Statistical Office of the EC, Luxembourg

the foreign tax system is relevant only to the extent that it affects the pre-tax rate of return. Although this heightens incentives to live and be taxed in a particular country, tax exiles are unlikely to become much more numerous purely because of a single currency. In short, tax rates on capital and income do not need to be equal within EMU.

2.1.4 The transmission mechanism

A country where changes in interest rates have effects similar to those in other EMU members will be a country that has less difficulty in living with a common monetary policy. The transmission mechanism of monetary policy in the UK is, however, far from average. The balance sheets of its households, companies, banks and building societies are significantly different from those in the main Continental economies. Personal debt is proportionately higher, and more of it is at variable interest rates. UK companies are similarly more dependent on floating-rate debt. And banks and building societies, which rely heavily on retail deposits paying variable rates, tend to have borrowing and lending rates that are closely linked to those set by the Bank of England. As a result, the effect of a rate change by the central bank comes through almost completely within a couple of months in the UK, whereas in Germany and Italy the impact is much smaller: after six months, only half the long-run effect has come through. In France, Denmark and Finland, the effects take even longer to materialize (see Cotarelli and Kourelis (1994) and Borio and Fritz (1994)).

A country where changes in interest rates have effects similar to those in other EMU members will be a country that has less difficulty in living with a common monetary policy.

For households, the most striking differences are in mortgage contracts. In the UK, only 15% of the outstanding mortgage debt is at fixed rates, which anyway tend to be fixed for less than four years. In Germany, just over 50% of mortgage debt is at rates that are completely fixed; in France, the figure is as much as 90%. Overall, in the UK about 80% of borrowing by the personal sector is at short-term or adjustable rates; in Germany that proportion is barely 40%, and in France it may even be lower. And the quantity of debt also varies: mortgage debt is around 60% of GDP in the UK, 40% in Germany, 25% in France, and less than 10% in Italy (see Miles (1994) and Borio (1994)). Simulations on macroeconomic models run by national central banks suggest that, for the UK, the impact of an interest rate change on domestic demand after two years is four times the EU average (see Bank for International Settlements (1994)).

Unless UK balance sheets become more European, inside EMU the UK would be more sensitive to changes in short-term interest rates.

The implication of all this is clear. Unless UK balance sheets become more European, inside EMU the UK would be more sensitive to changes in short-term interest rates. The impact of any change in European monetary policy would therefore be disproportionately channelled through the UK. As a result, the UK economy would be disproportionately volatile.

How should the government respond to such a prospect? That depends on two factors:

- Whether households and companies would naturally adjust their borrowing strategies.
- How unsuitable the ECB's interest rate might be for the UK.

Both are hard to gauge in advance, though it is surely unlikely that the interest rate set by the ECB would be more volatile than rates have been in the UK. The UK preference for floating rates is largely the child of its own inflation record over the past forty years. If inflation were to remain low and stable in EMU, the incentive to borrow and lend at fixed rates would rise. The yield curve for Euro government bonds might also be flatter than the sterling curve has been (another encouragement to longer-term, fixed-rate borrowing). It is, however, implausible that all this would happen quickly. It is wiser to assume that it will be a long time before the UK economy becomes no more sensitive to changes in monetary policy than the European average.

There are two types of policy that would speed up this adjustment. First, policies that encouraged a switch from variable to fixed-rate debt; secondly, policies to reduce debt gearing.

One way of assisting the first goal would be to set differential capital adequacy requirements for banks and building societies, favouring fixed-rate loans. If the risks of default on variable-rate debt (especially mortgages) rose as a result of short rates becoming less synchronized with the UK's cyclical position, it would be reasonable to require that more capital backed such loans. Such a move is consistent with current EU banking directives on capital adequacy, which specify minimum requirements but do not stop national supervisors from applying stricter rules.

As for reducing gearing, various tax changes would make debt relatively more expensive. Tax breaks for mortgages (MIRAS) and companies (full deductibility of interest payments from taxable income, but less generous treatment for equity funding) encourage debt financing. The benefits of MIRAS have been cut sharply

Table 2.6 Liabilities of non-financial enterprises as % total assets

Italy	76	(1994)
Norway	74	(1993)
Sweden	66	(1993)
Finland	64	(1993)
France	61	(1994)
Germany	60	(1994)
Spain	60	(1994)
Belgium	59	(1994)
Netherlands	56	(1993)
Denmark	54	(1994)
Austria	53	(1994)
UK	**38**	**(1994)**

Source: OECD Non-Financial Enterprises Financial Statements

over the past ten years, but the cost is still roughly £2.5 billion a year. If the UK is to join EMU, it would make sense to abolish MIRAS at the time of entry. The *de facto* loss to borrowers would be small, because the short-term Euro interest rate is likely to be below the rate that would exist if the UK stays out. Any boost to the government's finances would come at a time when, on macroeconomic grounds, a tightening in fiscal policy would be desirable anyway.

As for reducing gearing, various tax changes would make debt relatively more expensive. If the UK is to join EMU, it would make sense to abolish MIRAS.

Another way to reduce household gearing is to encourage new forms of finance for house purchase. One example is shared equity contracts, where lenders provide part of the funds to home buyers in the form of equity rather than debt. Another is shared appreciation mortgages, where lenders charge a lower interest rate (perhaps even zero) in exchange for sharing any gains in house value.

On the corporate side there would be less need for policies to reduce gearing. By European standards, UK companies are not highly leveraged (see Table 2.6). Nonetheless, ensuring that there is no bias against or in favour of either equity or debt financing, or between dividends and retentions, makes sense in its own right.

2.1.5 Funding

Inside EMU, all new issues of UK government bonds (gilts) would be denominated in Euros. If EMU membership were perceived to be irreversible, gilt yields would probably be no higher than the average yield on bonds issued by other EMU governments, since the UK's credit standing is better than average (see Table 4.1 on p. 41). This would mean that the real cost of servicing debt fell as two forces came into play:

1. In recent years, yields on UK medium dated gilts have been higher than the average yield on debt issued by those governments thought most likely to be in the single currency area; and that yield gap has exceeded the inflation gap. For example, during 1993–96 consumer price inflation in France averaged just under 2% a year, compared with 2.5% in the UK; yet in 1996 French bond yields were, on average, more than 150 basis points below gilt yields. Had markets been deriving their expectations of inflation from recent performance, the yield gap would have been half that size.

2. The demand for UK government debt denominated in Euros should be much larger than the demand for traditional gilts, since many institutional investors in Europe currently face restrictions on investing in foreign-currency assets.

Both factors should help to cut the real cost of servicing debt. But the impact on UK government finances would only build up slowly; even if all outstanding gilts were redenominated on EMU entry, the coupon payments on them would remain at the original values. Even after twenty years, there would probably still be a sizeable block of debt with real servicing costs higher than debt issued in Euros.

If the UK joins EMU, ownership of gilts is likely to become more international.

If the UK joins EMU, ownership of gilts is likely to become more international; currently less than 20% of the stock is held by foreigners. It might, therefore, be desirable to tailor the maturity pattern of new issues to the preferences of Continental investors. Hitherto, UK pension funds (whose liabilities tend to have long maturities) have provided a natural demand for long-dated bonds, so the average maturity of gilts has been substantially greater than in most other European countries. The sterling yield-curve has often been hump-shaped, with substantial demand at the very long end; large amounts of high maturity debt have been issued. If the Euro yield-curve did not dip down at the long end, it would be attractive to switch to more short and medium-term debt.

Inside EMU, that and other portfolio shifts are potentially huge. Tables 2.7 and 2.8 show the distributions of wealth (held directly by households, and by institutions on their behalf)

Table 2.7 Total gross financial assets ultimately owned by household sector, end 1995 (aggregation of direct asset holdings, pension fund assets, assets of insurance companies and funds in all collective investment schemes)

	$ billion	Value relative to annual GDP	% held directly by households	% held by pension funds (public and private)	% held by insurance companies	% held in collective investment schemes[a]
Austria	314	1.35	73	1	16	10
Canada	1313	2.30	60	20	12	8
Denmark	382	2.18	62	15	21	2
France	2972	1.91	62	2	18	17
Germany	3305	1.37	69	4	22	5
Italy	2140	2.05	85	3	8	4
Japan	12920	2.82	71	9	16	4
Norway	147	1.00	54	9	33	5
Spain	505	0.88	61	2	17	20
Sweden	342	1.38	24	27	38	11
Netherlands	747	1.89	20	45	28	7
UK	**3603**	**3.31**	**41**	**24**	**28**	**7**
US	23995	3.31	59	16	12	11

Note: [a] Unit trusts, investment trusts, mutual funds, etc.
Source: Merrill Lynch calculations based on Intersec data collected from national sources

Table 2.8 Portfolio allocation of total financial assets ultimately owned by the household sector, end 1995 (% of total aggregation of direct asset holdings, pension fund assets, assets of insurance companies and funds in all collective investment schemes)

	Cash & cash equivalents	Domestic bonds	Domestic equity	Foreign bonds	Foreign equity	Loans & mortgages	Real estate[a]	Other
Austria	8	25	26	4	8	6	1	21
Canada	32	18	31	1	6	6	1	5
Denmark	13	29	14	3	3	36	1	1
France	16	41	23	2	2	2	1	13
Germany	37	35	10	5	2	4	1	6
Italy	32	35	16	3	2	1	2	9
Japan	53	16	11	2	2	13	2	1
Norway	41	19	14	4	1	8	–	12
Spain	52	19	16	2	1	4	1	6
Sweden	14	45	26	1	6	3	3	1
Netherlands	8	19	14	6	10	38	5	1
UK	**22**	**10**	**44**	**3**	**13**	**0**	**3**	**4**
US	20	25	39	1	9	3	1	3

Note: [a] Real estate excludes direct ownership of residential property by households and includes only property held for investment purposes
Source: Merrill Lynch calculations based on Intersec data collected from national sources

across different financial assets at the end of 1995. In most Continental countries a higher proportion of wealth is held in bonds than in the UK, and nearly all of those bonds are issued by the domestic government. In the UK over 50% of financial assets are invested in equities, about one-quarter of which are in overseas equities. On the Continent equity holdings are generally nearer 20% of total financial wealth.

This pattern of portfolios will change in two ways inside EMU. First, for reasons already given, a Europe-wide switch towards buying more Euro-denominated gilts. Second, a switch out of UK equities. Assuming that Europe's desired holding of equities does not change in total, but that within each country there is a switch out of domestic equities and into equities of other 'ins', there will be a fall in the demand for the stocks of countries with relatively large equity markets. Over the longer term, however, the total demand for equities will probably grow as European countries switch to privately-funded pension schemes.

Before leaving the issue of funding, there is one other point to consider: the future of the UK's index-linked gilts, once they were denominated in Euros. Over the past ten years, indexed gilts have increased to about 20% of the outstanding stock. They have all been linked to the UK retail price index, and there is one strong argument for continuing this arrangement: UK pension funds and other long-term investors will still want to be protected against unanticipated shifts in the UK cost of living. There is, however, nothing to stop the UK government issuing debt linked to different price indices, so some experiments and market research may be useful.

With greater substitutability between the bonds issued by the various EMU governments, there will be more need to coordinate funding policy.

With greater substitutability between the bonds issued by the various EMU governments, there will be more need to coordinate funding policy. As a minimum that should cover the dates of auctions, but there is a strong case for coordinating maturities as well. Otherwise, several different countries could be launching large bond issues of the same maturity, providing an awkward kink in the Euro yield-curve.

2.1.6 The labour market

Inside EMU, macroeconomic policy will lose flexibility: that much is certain. How serious that is depends crucially on the structure of the labour market. If nominal wages are inflexible, then exogenous shocks will change real variables (employment and output). In a single currency area, a given degree of labour market inflexibility will become more costly in terms of lost jobs and output. But having flexible labour markets is desirable anyway[4]. Low marginal tax rates and a benefits system that does not discourage job creation are good things for every country. It is not obvious that EMU *per se* raises new policy issues for the UK labour market.

There may be one exception to this conclusion: the UK's tradition of wage bargaining, which produces settlements throughout the year. This is a form of nominal inertia, and its costs will rise inside EMU. To understand why, consider an open economy with nominal wage inertia. In this economy, devaluing the exchange rate is a means of coordinating a cut in real wages. Without the devaluation option, the same effect can be achieved only through coordinated wage settlements.

'Coordinated' wage bargaining can, however, have severe disadvantages of its own, particularly if it involves centralized control over the size (as opposed to just the timing) of pay increases. Plant-level agreements on pay and productivity have many benefits. And a partial move towards greater centralization might produce the worst of all worlds.

Coordinated wage bargaining also runs the risks of encouraging pressure to equalize wages across the single currency area. It will certainly be easier to compare wage levels once they are expressed in a common currency. Significant and sustained wage differentials reflect, however, differences in productivity; and since productivity levels are not likely to converge quickly, any rapid equalization of wages would damage employment in the poorer countries and regions of Europe.

It will certainly be easier to compare wage levels once they are expressed in a common currency. But any rapid equalization of wages would damage employment in the poorer countries and regions of Europe.

2.2 The UK as an 'out': longer term macroeconomic issues

2.2.1 The changing environment

As an 'out', the UK could continue to use all its existing policy instruments. In itself, this may seem an advantage; though the macroeconomic record over the past thirty years provides numerous examples of those instruments being misused. What is certain is that the wider context for macroeconomic management would change: living next door to an EMU with which the bulk of the UK's trade was conducted would have major ramifications. Most importantly, every UK government would need a credible policy on inflation, debt and deficits.

Assume, first, that EMU works well. The Euro would become the key currency for UK business, and a large proportion of its trade would be priced and paid for in Euros. Similarly, UK investors (and overseas investors holding UK financial assets) would view Euro-denominated assets as a natural part of their portfolios. Any perception that the UK would have higher and more variable inflation than the EMU countries, or generally laxer fiscal policy, would cause the demand for sterling assets to fall. The cost of falling asset prices and a declining exchange rate would be even higher than it has been traditionally.

Even if EMU works badly, the UK could suffer. EMU members would probably be particularly sensitive to the sterling-Euro rate, and prone to accuse the UK of stealing an unfair competitive advantage within the Single Market by devaluing the pound. The 'common concern' clause of the Maastricht Treaty means that EU countries that do not adopt the single currency are obliged to consider the knock-on effects for EMU members of any change in exchange rates. In a sense there is nothing new in this (EU countries outside the ERM are under a similar obligation) but the context will have changed. If EMU members no longer have their own national monetary policy to influence international competitiveness, they will be even more alert to the behaviour of others.

It would be far better for the UK to be seen as a sympathetic 'out' – 'out' because of its concern over its structural economic idiosyncrasies, but nonetheless committed to greater economic integration in Europe.

As always, perceptions of motive would count for a lot. It would be far better for the UK to be seen as a sympathetic 'out'; 'out' because of its concern over its structural economic idiosyncrasies, but nonetheless committed to greater economic integration in Europe. If the UK were seen as a carper and a blocker, wanting the benefits of the Single Market without the obligations of the single currency, it would surely suffer increasing discrimination from EMU members. In principle, overt discrimination is not allowed under the Maastricht Treaty and other EU laws. In practice, it is unworldly to suppose that discrimination is therefore impossible.

2.2.2   Policy instruments and targets

As an 'out', the key macroeconomic issues will centre on what policy targets to adopt and how to hit them.

1. If an inflation target is to be retained, how tight should it be?

2. Does it make sense to assign instruments to targets: having the Bank of England set interest rates to hit the inflation target, and setting tax and spending plans in a long-term context to control debt and deficits (and perhaps using intervention to try to influence the value of sterling)?

3. Should there be a target for the sterling-Euro exchange rate?

The ECB will aim to achieve price stability. Whether that will entail an explicit target for some particular price index (with target bands and dates) is still unclear. If there were, however, an explicit inflation target in EMU, it would have implications for the UK approach. For example, it would be difficult for the UK's inflation target to be higher than the ECB's without some loss of credibility. In itself, a gap that implied that UK inflation would, on average, be a percentage point or two above the EMU inflation rate might not be particularly damaging, especially if the ECB's monetary policy were seen to have erred on the side of tightness in the transitional period when it was seeking to establish credibility. But the gap might also invite other interpretations: that UK inflation would be much more variable, for example, or that a return to higher inflation was a distinct possibility.

Although the precise level of the UK inflation target would matter, the credibility of the means to achieve it would count for much more. The recent changes announced by the government giving operational independence to the Bank of England will be helpful.

Although the precise level of the UK inflation target would matter, the credibility of the means to achieve it would count for much more.

Of the other questions that arise in assigning instruments to targets, the most controversial is the possible adoption of an exchange-rate target. The previous section highlighted some of the dangers for the UK of sharp movements in the sterling-Euro rate, and to these should be added the possible damage to inward investment in the UK.

So some kind of exchange-rate stability would clearly be welcome. Wishful thinking, however, should not obscure the real difficulties of actually achieving stability. If the UK government were to adopt an exchange-rate target against the Euro, would this replace an inflation target, or be combined with it? If the latter, then these two targets would need two policy instruments. For all the reasons demonstrated by ERM experience, the interest rate need to keep inflation low would not necessarily be consistent with the exchange-rate target.

2.2.3   Fiscal policy and funding

For EMU members, the Stability Pact may have real bite, fining them if they run excessive deficits. As an 'out', the UK would not be subject to this threat. It is hard to see this as a disadvantage, so long as every future UK government was determined to run a prudent fiscal policy, and this determination was not questioned.

Preserving credibility would not require the UK to abide by the Stability Pact's ceiling of 3% of GDP. That limit is arbitrary and does not come from any calculation of long run sustainable policies. Nonetheless, it already has some symbolic significance. As a result, if any UK government did want to exceed the 3% limit, it would need to explain why; it would probably also need to stress that the move was temporary; and it would always need a longer-term framework of policies to ensure that the ratio of its total debt to GDP remained on a sustainable path. These require-ments would all become even more important than they now are, because investors in sterling assets (particularly gilts) would be much more inclined to switch into Euro-denominated assets.

If EMU produces low inflation and steady growth among its members, the Euro will undoubtedly become a major international currency, playing a role similar to the dollar.

The precise implications for funding will depend on a compar-ison between the success of EMU and that of an outsider economy like the UK's. If EMU produces low inflation and steady growth among its members, the Euro will undoubtedly become a major international currency, playing a role similar to the dollar. In that case, investors (both UK and foreign) may decide to switch some of their bond portfolios out of gilts. This would increase the UK government's cost of running budget deficits, at least if they are financed with sterling debt. Since only 4% of the UK's national debt is denominated in foreign currency, it might be wise to increase that through issuing Euro gilts. Any such decision will, however, depend on prevailing circumstances and likely prospects, so it is hard to lay down rules in advance.

At the other end of the spectrum, the markets may judge that the UK's performance as an 'out' looks much better than EMU's. Suppose that, within a few years of EMU's launch, strains between the 'ins' are so great that governments start to contem-plate the reintroduction of national currencies and interest rates. Even the possibility of that happening could cause a dramatic run into sterling and sterling-denominated assets. No UK government would or should be unaffected by such a develop-ment. As so often in the past, market pressure would require sharp changes in monetary and fiscal policy.

There is one other aspect of fiscal policy that is likely to be affected by EMU: the UK's net contribution to the central EU budget. Monetary union will bring pressure for a larger central budget, to finance fiscal transfers to cyclically depressed areas (though as we have already stressed, the economic validity of this case is questionable). It is unclear whether the UK as an 'out' would be excluded from this sort of EU activity. Any extra role for the EU budget will probably not be linked explicitly to a transfer fund for 'ins', so 'outs' may find it hard to avoid paying their share.

2.3 Competition policy and the Single Market

Joining a single currency would prevent the UK from using devaluation to protect UK firms from the consequences of their failure to compete. They would, therefore, have a greater incentive to survive by other means, fair or foul (including the attempt to shelter behind new forms of anti-competitive behaviour). Hence the importance of EU competition policy for both the Single Market and the single currency.

If the UK is 'in', the impact of EU competition policy will be fairly straightforward. UK firms will be subject to EU jurisdiction; the UK authorities will need to cooperate increasingly with Brussels; and the government will need to be satisfied that the implementation of competition policy is not distorted by political pressure from other member states. In all this, the most sensitive area will be state aid. In recent years, other EU governments have given much larger subsidies to industry than the UK has done (see Table 2.9), and the same is true of other forms of state protection.

In passing judgement on various forms of government assistance, the EU authorities' task will be made much harder if growth stays low and unemployment high. Governments might then argue that their subsidies were an essential part of counter-cyclical policy, designed to offset the effects of monetary restraint by the ECB. They could extend this claim to justify blocking take-overs of domestic firms by foreigners, appealing to what they might describe as 'exceptional difficulties' to prevent foreigners buying domestic assets at knock-down prices owing to the recession.

Table 2.9 State aid to the manufacturing sector. Annual averages 1990–92 and 1988–90

	in per cent of value added		in ECU per person employed	
	1988–90	**1990–92**	**1988–90**	**1990–92**
Belgium	5.0	4.3	1744	1527
Denmark	2.3	2.0	685	638
former Germany[a]	2.6	2.1	1099	979
new Länder		N/A		4385
Greece	16.9	12.3	2420	1579
Spain	3.7	1.7	1080	493
France	3.7	3.0	1449	1138
Ireland	3.9	2.9	1821	1411
Italy	7.8	8.9	2425	2611
Luxembourg	3.4	4.1	1369	1573
Netherlands	3.2	2.6	1466	978
Portugal	7.3	5.2	911	625
UK	**1.9**	**1.5**	**756**	**525**
EUR 12	3.8	3.7	1372	1293

Note: [a] in its borders before October 1990
Source: European Commission, 'Fourth Survey on State Aid in the EU in the Manufacturing and Certain Other Sectors', 1995

After sterling withdrew from the ERM, some EU members put considerable pressure on the Commission to relax EU rules on state aid for firms that had suffered as a result of 'competitive devaluations'.

All these difficulties could arise even if the UK is 'in'. If it is 'out', however, there is an extra complication since the 'ins' may claim that it is using its exchange rate to gain an 'unfair' advantage and therefore adding to their 'exceptional difficulties'. There is no good economic case for such a view, but that may not prevent it from being very influential. After sterling withdrew from the ERM in 1992, some EU members put considerable pressure on the Commission to relax EU rules on state aid for firms that had suffered as a result of 'competitive devaluations'. The Commission resisted making an explicit concession, but the pressure may influence decisions in particular cases.

Those decisions do ultimately entail considerable discretion for the EU state authorities. The rules on state aid are governed by Article 92(1) of the 1957 EC Treaty:

Save as otherwise provided in the Treaty, any aid granted by a member State or through State resources in any form whatsoever which distorts or threatens to distort competition by favouring certain undertakings or the production of certain goods shall, in so far as it affects trade between member States, be incompatible with the common market.

The notions of 'distortion' of competition and the 'favouring' of 'certain undertakings' or 'certain goods' have been interpreted in many different ways. They could be used not only to justify state aid by 'ins' but also to ban certain policies of the 'outs' (towards inward investment in poorer regions, for example). Although the Single Market Act seeks to outlaw actions that discriminate against firms from an 'out' country, in reality ambiguity abounds. Article 19 of the Maastricht Treaty gives member states the right to act 'in the general good'. Any action by an 'out' that could be seen as making the operation of monetary policy more difficult in EMU could be deemed to be against the general good, and therefore provide a pretext for discrimination to support the general good.

Discrimination takes many forms and comes in subtle shades. For example, UK firms that hoped to do business in markets where regulatory barriers are still significant (telecoms, public utilities) might find those barriers stayed up longer if the UK were 'out'. The whole area of public procurement also gives national governments significant power to discriminate, and to produce justifications for doing so. For instance, an 'in' government could argue that a company from an 'out' country faced currency risks that might prevent it from fulfilling its contractual obligations.

All this may be specious, petty and disgraceful, but name-calling does not change the fact that such behaviour is common (and not just in the EU). All international companies know that there is hardly a country in the world where the playing field is truly level. The bias towards domestic firms may be small or large, covert or overt; it is very rarely absent.

The surest way for the UK to minimize discrimination against UK-based firms is to participate actively in the development of the Single Market. If the UK stays out of EMU, this participation will be even more important (and perhaps more difficult too). Much will depend on attitude. If the UK is seen as a constructive agnostic on EMU, it will be listened to on subjects such as competition policy. If it comes across as a whingeing outsider, it won't.

The surest way for the UK to minimize discrimination against UK-based firms is to participate actively in the development of the Single Market.

3

The institutional framework

3.1 The Bank of England

If the UK joins EMU, it will first have to make the Bank of England independent. The government plans to introduce legislation later this year to give the Bank operational independence over monetary policy; under the new regime the government will set an inflation target and the Bank will set interest rates to hit it. It is intended that in exceptional circumstances, and only with the approval of parliament, the government will have the power to give instructions to the Bank on interest rates for a limited period.

Although the planned legislation would create a more independent central bank it will fall short of the requirements of the Maastricht Treaty.

Although this planned legislation will create a more independent central bank, it will fall short of the requirements of the Maastricht Treaty. Further amendments to the statutes of the Bank of England are likely to be necessary if the UK is to join EMU. And if it wants to be in EMU's first wave, it will have to move very fast. The European Monetary Institute (EMI) will produce its report on convergence early in 1998, and it must be convinced that legislation consistent with full central bank independence will be in place by the time the European System of Central Banks (ESCB) comes into being in January 1999.

Article 107 of the Maastricht Treaty sets out what central bank independence means. The key requirement is that national central banks should neither seek nor take instruction from Community institutions or bodies, from any government of a member state, or from any other body. The EMI interprets the Article to mean that the following rights of third parties (including governments and parliaments) are incompatible with the Treaty:

1. Rights to give instructions to the national central bank (NCB).

2. Rights to approve, suspend, annul or defer decisions.

3. Rights to censor decisions on legal grounds.

4. Rights to participate in decision-making bodies of an NCB with a right to vote.

5. Rights to be consulted on an NCB's decisions.

Clearly the degree of independence required is, in important respects, inconsistent with the role of government and of parliament outlined by the UK government when it announced operational independence of the Bank of England.

The EMI believes that the statutes of NCBs need to guarantee that the Governor of the central bank has a term of office of five years or more, and can be dismissed only for failure to fulfil his or her duties. Furthermore:

Personal independence could be jeopardised if the same rules for the security of tenure of office of Governors were not also applied to other members of the decision-making bodies of NCBs involved in the performance of ECB-related tasks.

(EMI's 'Progress Towards Convergence' report, November 1996.)

The statutes of an independent central bank also need to specify its functions in a way that is consistent with the Treaty: explicit primacy for the maintenance of price stability and financial independence. The EMI interprets this last point as follows:

Ex ante influence on an NCB's financial needs may infringe an NCB's independence. In those countries where third parties, particularly the government and/or parliament, are in a position, directly or indirectly, to exercise influence on the determination of an NCB's budget or the distribution of profit, the relevant statutory provisions should contain a safeguard clause to ensure that this does not impede the proper performance of the NCB's ESCB-related tasks.

For EMU membership, a new Bank of England statute would also have to be consistent with Article 104 of the Maastricht Treaty. This prohibits the provision of central-bank credit to the public sector or the granting of privileged access by government or public bodies to financial institutions. The new law would also lay down that competence for monetary policy is transferred from the government to lie exclusively with the Governing Council of the ECB, and that the Bank of England becomes an integral part of the ESCB and shares its function as being primarily concerned with price stability.

A new statute for the Bank of England will of course be controversial, and not just because it is required for EMU.

Some of these detailed issues, particularly the question of the financial independence of the Bank, are inherently tricky. The EMI argues that an ex-post review of a central bank's financial accounts by the government could be regarded as a 'reflection of an NCB's accountability towards its owners' but only 'provided that the NCB's statute contains adequate safeguards that such a review will not infringe its independence'. Quite how accountability of the central bank to its owners is squared with a high degree of independence is an awkward corner that would have to be negotiated by the drafters of any legislation intended to make the Bank of England a Maastricht-complaint body.

Even if the government decides to miss the first EMU wave, it will still have to recognize that something beyond operational independence for the Bank is likely to be a precondition of later entry. In that case, it could not delay the introduction of further legislation on the statutes of the Bank for long, because the same complexities will have to be faced.

What if the government decides to stay out of EMU? In that case, assuming that the inflation objectives set for the Bank are similar to those that currently exist, there is no compelling reason to go beyond the new plans to grant operational independence to the Bank. The retention of a government override (in exceptional circumstances and only with parliamentary approval) to Bank control over interest rates and the requirement for the Bank to make reports and give evidence to the House of Commons are important elements in creating accountability.

3.2 The operation of monetary policy

The operational (as opposed to macroeconomic) implications of having monetary policy decided by the ECB and then implemented by national central banks are, with one exception, not particularly profound. As an 'in', the UK's open market operations would be conducted by the Bank of England on terms consistent with the monetary policy decided by the ECB. Repurchase agreements (repos) are almost certain to be the main form of operation, as they have recently become in the UK. Although there is some uncertainty about what instruments will count as eligible assets for repo, the conduct of operations does not raise any real policy issues.

The exception to this is the issue of reserve requirements. Several central banks (notably the Bundesbank) regard reserve requirements as an essential tool of monetary policy. Others (notably the Bank of England) disagree. The EMI is still discussing whether reserve requirements will be set by the ECB, but has not reached a conclusion. Any discussion of their implications is therefore unavoidably tentative, and we will restrict ourselves to a few basic points.

- If reserve requirements carry interest rates that are below market rates, they act as a tax on the intermediation of funds through the balance sheets of banks.

- Their economic impact depends on how easily they can be avoided by borrowers and lenders (disintermediation), and what impact that has.

- As an initial 'in', the UK would be better able to influence how reserve requirements were used and might be able to minimize their impact.

- As an 'out', the UK (more precisely, the City of London) would gain if financial institutions try to avoid ECB reserve requirements by channelling business through London.

- But this might provoke retaliation from EMU members on the grounds that the UK was undermining the ECB's monetary policy.

- Should measures be taken to prevent disintermediation? In itself, disintermediation may not seem very desirable, partly because it makes monetary and credit aggregates hard to read. But it does reduce the economic distortions stemming from an undesirable tax. The root of the problem is the tax; disintermediation is merely a symptom.

As an initial 'in', the UK would be better able to influence how reserve requirements were used and might be able to minimize their impact.

3.3 TARGET

TARGET is the system for real time gross settlements (RTGS) that will be operated by the ECB. It will link together national systems and allow real time settlement in Euros. If the UK stays out of the first wave, it will face the question of the terms on which UK institutions can use TARGET. In particular can they get intra-day liquidity (in Euros) from the ECB so as to make payments? Some of EMU's first-wave candidates say that this should not be allowed, but their arguments are confusing. Provided intra-day liquidity does not spill over into overnight loans, it is hard to see any monetary policy implications of granting intra-day loans to institutions from 'out' countries.

It is unclear how this issue will be settled. If banks from 'out' countries want to use TARGET but are denied access to intra-day liquidity, they will have to hold more liquid assets than banks from 'in' countries. This is a disadvantage. But there are alternatives to using TARGET that will be available and will probably not be much more expensive. Banks from 'out' countries could use correspondent banks. They could also set up branches or subsidiaries in EMU countries and then use TARGET via them. Even if neither approach is feasible, the need to hold extra liquid assets generates extra costs only to the extent that the return on those assets is less than a market rate.

3.4 Supervision and the lender-of-last-resort

The statutes of the European Central Bank give it no responsibility for supervising financial institutions. Nor do they say that the ECB should be lender-of-last-resort. From one point of view, this silence seems puzzling: if there ever were a need to provide support to banks to prevent systemic risk, surely the ECB could not fail to be involved at some level? It has sole responsibility for monetary policy, and any operation to provide liquidity on a large scale is bound to have monetary policy implications.

If there ever were a need to provide support to banks to prevent systemic risk, surely the ECB could not fail to be involved at some level?

From that starting point, it seems natural to conclude that the ECB should have a role in supervision. After all, any judgements on how much liquidity to make available and on what terms will depend on gauging the solvency of key institutions and possible knock-on effects. That kind of assessment requires familiarity with the institutions: ergo, the ECB should be supervisor.

The case against the ECB as supervisor starts with the point that national supervisors are already familiar with individual banks, and they will always be closer to their local conditions than any supranational body could be. Between these two positions lies the possibility of a compromise. Much of the formal supervision currently undertaken at the national level is likely to remain there, though it may be conducted within a set of common (minimum) requirements. This would be little more than today's status quo, in which European Banking

Directives (e.g. on capital adequacy) are administered by national supervisors.

Some parallels with the United States are instructive. There, the Federal Reserve Board formally has authority over the Federal Reserve Banks for banking supervision and the use of the discount window. But supervision is actually done by the Reserve Banks. They employ most of the supervisors, and it is they that make discount window loans on their own books. They are not merely the means for implementing Board policy on supervision; they are themselves heavily involved in making policy.

There are therefore strong operational grounds for leaving supervision in the hands of national authorities. And if they are not convincing, there is a quasi-constitutional reason as well. In many European countries, including the UK, banking supervision is done by a national authority with responsibility to a Minister (of Finance) and ultimately to parliament. If the ECB were to take over supervision, to what would it be accountable? Presumably to the European Commission, or the Council, or the European parliament. That would, however, complicate (if not undermine) its independence on monetary policy. It is no accident that the Maastricht Treaty gives no supervisory powers to the ESCB, since its statutes are designed to match the Bundesbank's. The Bundesbank has no role in supervision, primarily because of the perceived risk of a conflict between the goals of monetary policy and supervision.

It is no accident that the Maastricht Treaty gives no supervisory powers to the ESCB, since its statutes are designed to match the Bundesbank's.

All in all, supervisory systems are most unlikely to change much, in or out of EMU. But this conclusion invites a closer look at the lender-of-last-resort issue. One version of this role is the support that a central bank gives to specific financial institutions that are unable to obtain credit from other sources, and whose failure could trigger systemic weakness. In such cases, a national central bank could make a loan to the distressed institution on its own book. If indeed that loan was not repaid in full, then the central bank would face losses which would ultimately be borne by the national government.

A second type of lender-of-last-resort function comes when a central bank injects extra liquidity into the whole financial system. If the ECB did not like the implication for monetary policy, it could offset the effects through its open market operations. In EMU, that could be done only by the ECB. It alone can create Euro liquidity, by injecting more reserves into the system or by reducing lending rates (or, if there are reserve requirements, by relaxing them).

In the real world, unfortunately, the response to banking difficulties seldom falls neatly into one category or the other. The example of Barings is a recent illustration. In February 1995, the UK government and the Bank of England decided not to support Barings; but at the same time, in order to prevent any contagion for others, the Bank announced that it was ready to provide liquidity to the banking system as a whole. Inside EMU, the national authorities could still decide whether or not to support a particular bank with their own capital. But what they could not do, at least not without first convincing the Governing Council of the ECB, is provide more liquidity to the money markets so as to prevent contagion.

Inside EMU, the national authorities could still decide whether or not to support a particular bank with their own capital.

Our review so far has excluded one other possibility: that the supervisory system is anyway likely to change fundamentally, both functionally and geographically. There is a growing sense in the UK and elsewhere that the supervisory split between banks and security firms makes less and less sense as financial institutions increasingly combine both activities. Equally, as financial institutions become more international in their business, supervisors have to look beyond national borders in order to do their job properly.

It is beyond the scope of this report to go into this possibility thoroughly. It is enough to say that it is not logically or necessarily a function of being in or out of EMU. The issue will probably arise anyway. EMU can hasten the day, but no more than that.

3.5   International organizations: G7 or G3?

G7 meetings to discuss the world economy and macro-economic policies take place at regular intervals. The Finance Ministers of the seven countries are there, with their central bank Governors. The European members are Germany, France, Italy and the UK. Once the ECB is set up, it is clear that its President will attend the G7. He may replace the Governors of whichever countries are in EMU, except that that would create the rather bizarre situation where the Governors of (say) the Bank of England and the Banca d'Italia are there, whereas the President of the Bundesbank and the Governor of the Banque de France are not. As for fiscal policy, only if it became almost completely centralized would it be likely that a single

European representative replaced the Finance Ministers of the four European countries.

Whatever happens, the advent of EMU will change the tidy arrangements for G7 meetings. Charles Goodhart (1995) puts it this way:

After EMU there will need to be at least five attendants from the EC on fiscal policy matters (the four major Ministers from the large member states and an EC Commission representative) and a completely separate independent representative from the ESCB to discuss monetary matters (with whom? The Federal Reserve Board or with the Ministers of Finance?) The chain of command and relative responsibility are almost certain to become more muddled, even than now, and the number of people sitting around the table will not fall by much. Instead of the G7 being a discussion among politicians in exactly the same positions in national governments, it will become a mixture of federal and national politicians with fiscal responsibilities and a melange of politicians and Central Bankers with widely varying degrees of responsibility for monetary policies[5].

This does not sound very durable. Sooner or later, the G7 system will change, if only to reflect the profound shift in the world's economic geography over the past 30 years. Again, EMU itself will not cause the change, but it may well be the catalyst. In the process, it is hard to see how the UK will retain its seat at a small top table, though a bigger table would be more accommodating.

Sooner or later, the G7 system will change, if only to reflect the profound shift in the world's economic geography over the past 30 years.

4

Timing

When is the right time to decide about EMU? If parliament and the electorate want the UK to be in EMU, when is the right time to join? Does a strategy of wait and see make sense? If so, how long should the wait last, and what needs to be done soon to keep the various options open? These are big questions, with big implications. So far, the UK debate has all but ignored them.

Broadly, there are two dimensions to each of these questions.

- **The current macroeconomic conjuncture**. Should the exchange rates and cyclical positions of the UK and the first-wave candidates affect the UK's judgement about joining and the timing of announcing a decision?

- **Lead times**. If the UK is to join EMU, how long would it take to do the things that are either necessary (e.g. full central bank independence) or desirable (e.g. making the transmission mechanism more like the rest of Europe)?

4.1 The conjuncture

This report has so far discussed how fiscal policy, tax systems, competition policy, funding strategy and policy institutions might need to be different once the UK either was in EMU or clearly out. But there will of course be a period of transition, and it raises different questions. It will not be brief, since it includes the phase leading up to the start of EMU (at least eighteen months), the early years of the ECB and (if the government decides to join in the second wave) the UK's time in the waiting room.

In considering this transition period, the government cannot ignore four factors in particular:

4.1.1   The exchange rate

First, setting the exchange rate between sterling and the Euro will be crucial. When sterling left the ERM in 1992, its trade-weighted value depreciated by about 14%. The real effects of this depreciation (on the profitability of UK exports and the competitiveness of imports) were not neutralized by sharp increases in domestic wages. As a result, export volumes increased strongly and the UK's economic growth moved up while most Continental economies remained depressed. More recently though, sterling has returned towards ERM levels and the opposite consequences have begun to make themselves felt (see Figure 4.1).

This suggests that it would be a serious mistake to link sterling to the Euro at anything like its current cross rate against the Deutsche Mark block. Suppose, however, that the UK announced that it wanted to aim to join the first wave, how would this affect the exchange rate? The outcome would depend crucially on the perceived strategies that the UK government, and the other 'ins', were going to follow in the lead up to EMU. It is possible that other 'ins' would say that they would like the final conversion rates to be close to the ERM central parities; if credible, this announcement would tend to force rates towards those levels during 1998. As Figure 4.1 shows, there has been little variation in the bilateral exchange rates of some of the ERM countries against the Deutsche Mark, so a commitment to be at the central parities at the end of 1998 would be taken seriously. Unless the UK rejoined the ERM that particular option would not be open

Setting the exchange rate between sterling and the Euro will be crucial.

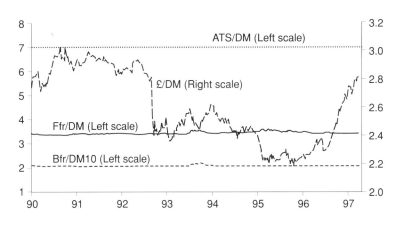

Figure 4.1   Deutsche Mark exchange rates
Key: Exchange rates
Ffr/DM = French franc/ Deutsche Mark
Bfr/DM10 = $\frac{1}{10}$ of Belgium franc/Deutsche Mark

to it. Even so, the markets might be persuaded to believe that the UK and other EU countries were going to engineer a decline in sterling, down to a rate that broadly reflected relative prices of tradeable goods. In that case, the perception might be self-fulfilling. But less palatable outcomes are clearly possible. The economic costs of being locked forever to an exchange rate that was significantly overvalued may not themselves be permanent; but history suggests that they would last long enough to do substantial cumulative damage.

This danger is exacerbated by the Maastricht Treaty rule that joiners will have their exchange rates converted at the market rate just one day before entry. If the UK has no alternative but to accept this, it would clearly be desirable either to manage the exchange rate down or else to announce the decision to join in principle but wait until the exchange rate is at an acceptable level before quickly going in.

During the transition phase, the UK would be required to consider sterling's rate against the Euro as a matter of 'common concern' to EU members. It may also face pressure to join the exchange rate mechanism (ERM), a point that requires some elaboration. Obviously it would not now be possible for sterling to be in the ERM for two years leading up to a January 1999 start for EMU. But a two-year stint would be possible if the UK delays entry. Strictly interpreted, the entry conditions for EMU seem to require ERM membership first. The UK government has argued that the precondition that matters is currency stability, not the institutional mechanism through which stability is achieved. But

If the UK were determined that sterling should not fluctuate by more than the wide bands of the ERM against the Euro, why should it want to stay outside the ERM?

if the UK was determined that sterling should not fluctuate by more than the wide bands of the ERM (plus or minus 15% from the central parity) against the Euro in the period between 1999 and entry, why should it want to stay outside the ERM? This is a question asked by some EU governments and officials. It has not yet been properly resolved, perhaps reflecting the Continental sense that the UK was not really serious about joining EMU anyway.

4.1.2 The boost to bonds

Over the past two years, yields on medium-dated German government bonds have, on average, been 150 basis points below those on UK gilts. That differential would fall sharply as it became clear that the UK would be 'in' from the start. As an 'in', UK gilts would be unlikely to trade at much of a premium

Table 4.1 EU – sovereign ratings, end 1996

	Foreign			Domestic		
	Moody's	S&P	IBCA	Moody's	S&P	IBCA
Austria	Aaa	AAA	AAA	–	AAA	AAA
Belgium	Aa1	AA+	AA+	–	AAA	AAA
Denmark	Aa1	AA+	AA+	Aaa	AAA	AAA
Finland	Aa2	AA–(+)	AA	Aaa	AAA	AAA
France	Aaa	AAA	AAA	Aaa	AAA	AAA
Germany	Aaa	AAA	AAA	Aaa	AAA	AAA
Greece	Baa1	BBB–	BBB–	–	–	–
Ireland	Aa2	AA	AA+	Aaa	AAA	AAA
Italy	Aa3	AA+(–)	AA–	Aa3	AAA	AAA
Luxembourg	Aaa	AAA	AAA	–	AAA	AAA
Netherlands	Aaa	AAA	AAA	–	AAA	AAA
Portugal	A1	AA–	AA–	–	AAA	AAA
Spain	Aa2	AA	AA	–	AAA	AAA
Sweden	Aa3	AA+(–)	AA–	Aa1	AAA	AAA
UK	**Aaa**	**AAA**	**AAA**	**Aaa**	**AAA**	**AAA**

Note: (+) indicates positive outlook   (–) indicates negative outlook

over French or German government bonds, since country credit ratings (see Table 4.1) are identical.

The price of ten-year bonds might therefore rise by 10% or more, generating huge capital gains. Outstanding gilts total over £300 billion, so the wealth gain for UK investors could be around £30 billion. Equities are harder to predict, but would probably rise too. In short, through the effects on financial assets, an 'in' announcement would give a big boost to spending power. At the same time, monetary conditions would ease as long interest rates fell; and prospective short rates may also be lower, because the ECB may initially set interest rates to suit economies with slower growth and higher unemployment.

4.1.3 Unsynchronized cycles

The previous two paragraphs lead on to the major question of cyclical differences between the UK and other EMU candidates. The UK economy has been growing solidly for four years, and unemployment has already fallen sharply. By contrast, growth in the rest of the EU has been sluggish and unemployment is still rising (see Figures 4.2 and 4.3). It is hard to see any single macroeconomic policy that can reconcile the needs of two such different conjunctures (and the problems may get worse before

The UK economy has been growing solidly for four years, and unemployment has already fallen sharply. By contrast, growth in the EU has been sluggish and unemployment is still rising.

Figure 4.2 EU real GDP (Average 1992–96, % year on year)

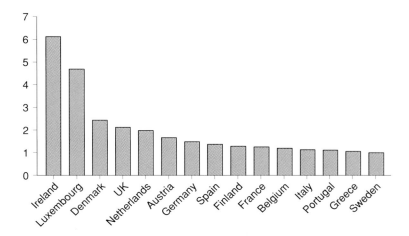

they could get better). In 1998, UK preparation for membership would have to include three goals: getting the exchange rate down; preventing domestic overheating; and reducing the fiscal deficit. Only when these had been achieved could the UK cyclical position begin to resemble the rest of the EU's.

The real difficulty is that there are too many targets relative to instruments, and this would obviously get worse in EMU, when interest rates will be set by the ECB. It may, therefore, be necessary for UK fiscal policy to be *much* tighter in the period before the Euro is established, and for a few years afterwards, than would be the case if the UK stayed out. The mere act of joining a single currency area does not prevent inflationary pressures varying significantly from country to country.

Figure 4.3 EU unemployment (Percent)

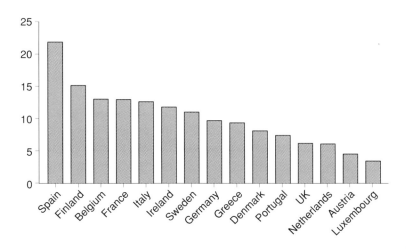

4.1.4 On the sidelines

Even with the right exchange rate, and with the economy and institutions ready for membership, it may still be prudent to stay out for a while. In the ECB's first few years, it will face formidable problems in setting interest rates. It will want to establish its anti-inflation credentials at a time when the demand for Euros (both domestic and from abroad) will be unpredictable. This will make the monetary aggregates hard to fathom and the Euro's exchange rate very volatile.

Some may feel that staying on the sidelines will create a free-rider problem: not everyone can have a 'wait and see' strategy, and those who join in the first tricky phase will resent the UK's faint-hearted approach. In practice, the free-rider problem can be exaggerated. After all, there is no shortage of countries wanting to be in EMU from the start.

4.2 Lead times

If the UK wants to join EMU, how long will it take to lay the ground for entry, so as to meet all the system's requirements and minimize the possible costs of joining?

It is easy to underestimate the time that will be needed. Politically, all the main parties are committed to a referendum on EMU membership. Institutionally, the Bank of England must become fully independent. Economically, the UK cycle should ideally be synchronized with the rest of the EU. Fiscally, the budget deficit should be cut, and put on a credible path towards surplus. All of these steps have, in varying degrees, been taken by other members of the EU. The UK has done virtually nothing about any of them.

Of course it makes no economic sense to postpone entry until all these changes have been made. In particular, it would be illogical to wait until every aspect of the UK transmission mechanism was identical to that in other EU countries. A government that wants to join EMU does so because it thinks the benefits will outweigh the costs. For it, each year outside means losing some benefits. As we made clear at the beginning, our report does not provide a full cost-benefit analysis of EMU. It merely seeks to establish the policy implications of whatever is decided about EMU, so it has a natural bias to emphasize costs and downplay benefits. The remaining few pages now bring all the points together.

It would be illogical to wait until every aspect of the UK transmission mechanism was identical to that in other EU countries.

5

The ways ahead

The UK government has four possible strategies for EMU:

1. Join at the start.

2. Decide to join, but do so later.

3. Wait and see. The pragmatic agnostic's position: if EMU works, then join at some unspecified date.

4. Decide in principle not to join.

This final section considers the implications of our analysis for the policies that should be adopted under each of the four strategies. Table 5.1 on p. 49 summarizes what is to be done.

5.1 Join at the start

This is a very ambitious timetable. For practical reasons, it may even be impossible. It will require the following steps:

■ **A fully independent central bank by the end of 1998**. This would involve primary, and complex, legislation. The government would therefore have to attach high priority to drafting and passing a new Bank of England Act that was in important respects different from that outlined by the Chancellor when on May 6th 1997 he announced his plans to give the Bank operational independence.

■ **Tighten fiscal policy immediately**. This requirement would not be driven primarily by the limit of 3% for the deficit to GDP ratio, but by the need to tighten macroeconomic policy before the UK was subject to an interest rate that would probably be much lower than it needs for its current cyclical state. Interest rates in EMU's first-wave candidates are now 3% below UK rates, and the gap might be wider in a year's time. To stop the economy from overheating, fiscal policy must be tightened. Given the time lags, the tightening should be large and immediate. And since EMU members will want some flexibility to ease fiscal policy as a counter-cyclical measure without running up against the 3% limit, it would be wise to use the economy's current strength to aim for a surplus within a few years of EMU's launch.

To stop the economy from overheating, fiscal policy must be tightened. Given the time lags, the tightening should be large and immediate.

- **A lower exchange rate**. If EMU starts on time, bilateral exchange rates will be permanently fixed between the initial 'ins' at the end of 1998. Between now and then, sterling must depreciate against the Deutsche Mark to something like purchasing power parity; otherwise, the real economy will be severely damaged by the early years of EMU membership. Perhaps a depreciation will happen automatically as fiscal policy is tightened. Otherwise, the rate should be talked down; if that fails, it should be sold down.

- **Enhancing automatic fiscal stabilisers**, to compensate for the loss of autonomy over monetary policy.

- **Reducing the tax incentive to use debt**. This will help make the transmission mechanism of UK monetary policy more like that in other EMU candidates.

These last two recommendations are really longer-term strategies, but they will take time to bear fruit. The sooner they can be adopted the better.

5.2 Decide to join, but later

A decision to delay entry by, say, three or four years would ease or eliminate the practical problems of the first-wave timetable. It will not be imperative to make the Bank of England fully independent by the end of 1998, though legislation should not be delayed for long. It will also be desirable to bring in legislative measures to enhance the fiscal stabilisers; they will then have a chance to start working.

By 2001 or 2002 the EMU interest rate may well be broadly what the UK economy needs in the cyclical circumstances it will then find itself.

But the bigger advantages of delay relate to conjunctural and exchange rate concerns. By 2001 or 2002 the EMU interest rate may well be broadly what the UK economy needs in the cyclical circumstances it will then find itself. But the benefits of joining EMU with a small budget surplus would still apply, so fiscal policy ought to be set on a path to achieve it. As for the exchange rate, who knows? 'In' or 'out' of the ERM, at least the goal of bringing the sterling-Euro rate close to fundamental (purchasing power parity) rates could be tackled over a longer period.

5.3   Wait and see

EMU is a project without precedent. Nobody knows how it will work. Nor can anybody be sure that the UK is a suitable member. The theologians of the EMU debate either want to be in (and sooner rather than later) or they do not want to join at all, ever. The pragmatic agnostic merely says that there are a lot of uncertainties at the moment, but many of these will be resolved one way or another over the next few years. Better to wait and see.

Even on this view, though, there are policy changes to be made now. Some would be helpful regardless of the UK's eventual decision on EMU. Others would be desirable if the Euro were ultimately to be adopted, but otherwise are less clearly helpful. The first category includes:

■ Making the tax treatment of debt and equity more equal. This involves abolishing MIRAS and reducing the tax disincentives for companies to use equity and retain profits.

■ Reducing the fiscal deficit. On cyclical grounds the deficit is currently too large. Structurally too, the long-term spending and revenue prospects are uncomfortably out of balance. It would be useful to set fiscal policy on a path to generate cyclically adjusted balances between spending and revenues that were, on average, no greater than public sector investment.

A second category of measures would be less obviously helpful if in fact the UK never did join EMU.

■ Enhancing the size of the automatic fiscal stabilisers.

- Increasing fiscal flexibility – for example, by making the timing of tax payments depend on macroeconomic conditions.

Under a wait and see strategy there is an issue about the nature of central bank independence. As we have noted several times, the kind of independence that the Maastricht Treaty requires goes beyond that which the Chancellor's announcement of May 6th 1997 suggests will be established by the proposed amendment to the Bank of England Act of 1946. It follows that a further amendment to that Act would appear to be necessary in order for the UK to qualify for membership. But there may be an alternative; it is conceivable that the legislation to amend the Bank of England Act could include in it clauses which allow that in the event of a decision to join EMU the arrangements between the Bank, government and parliament would be changed in ways consistent with the Maastricht blueprint for the statutes of a national central bank.

It is conceivable that the legislation to amend the Bank of England Act could include in it clauses which allow that in the event of a decision to join a monetary union the relation between the Bank, government and parliament be changed.

5.4 Never join

If this were the decision, publicly announced and unambiguous, the policy imperative would be to bolster credibility. The markets would need persuading that a UK out on its own was not a UK that would return to its old inflationary ways. The most persuasive step of all is the establishment of an independent bank, so the measures recently announced by the Chancellor are clearly helpful.

Of the other possible measures, reducing the current fiscal deficit would also be valuable. Similarly, reducing the tax incentives for the use of debt is desirable in its own right. But with continuing control over domestic interest rates, there is no compelling reason for enhancing the role for automatic fiscal stabilisers.

With an independent Bank of England and an autonomous monetary policy, one new factor would start to loom large. The sterling-Euro exchange rate would be much more important for UK business than any bilateral rate now is. Sharp fluctuations in the rate would be more damaging than a similar fluctuation in a bilateral rate today. This is partly because 60% or more of UK trade would be invoiced in Euros, and also because countries inside EMU would not be able to adjust their exchange rate against the UK.

The exchange rate would therefore have great potential, for good or bad. But the context in which it moved would also matter. If the UK stays out of EMU, will its politicians sound as though they want to be out of wider EU decisions as well? If so, EMU members will not regard the Euro's exchange rate with sterling as a purely market-driven technicality. It will increasingly become a pretext for arguing with the UK, and perhaps discriminating against UK companies.

EMU ought to be an economic issue, though so far it has largely been driven by politics. In the longer term, it will be even harder to keep the politics out of EMU, unless all concerned realize the damage that could do. 'In' or 'out', the UK would do well to keep the political temperature down.

If the UK stays out of EMU, will its politicians sound as though they want to be out of wider EU decisions as well?

Table 5.1 EMU – the policy options

	Tighten fiscal policy immediately and substantially	Aim for fiscal surplus by 2001	Enhance automatic fiscal stabilisers	Establish fully independent[a] Bank of England by end of 1998	Establish operational independence for the Bank of England	Change tax system to reduce incentives to use debt	Prevent DM/£ rate deviating substantially from fundamental value in 1998	Prevent Euro/£ rate deviating substantially from fundamental value
1. Aim to join EMU at the start	✓	✓	✓	✓	N/A	●	✓	N/A
2. Aim to join EMU some time later	●	✓	✓	●	✓	●	x	●
3. Keep option open to join: 'wait and see'	●	●	?	?	✓	●	x	●
4. No intention to join EMU	●	x	x	x	●	●	x	●

Key: ✓ Essential   x Not recommended
● Desirable but not essential   N/A Not applicable
Note: [a] i.e. consistent with Maastricht blueprint for the statutes of a national central bank

Further reading

Bayoumi, T. and Eichengreen, B. (1996) 'Operationalizing the Theory of Optimum Currency Areas', CEPR Discussion Paper No. 1484, October.

Bank for International Settlements (1994) *Financial Structure and the Monetary Policy Transmission Mechanism* (Basle).

Borio (1994) 'The Structure of Credit to the Non-Government Sector and the Transmission Mechanism of Monetary Policy', Bank for International Settlements working paper No. 24.

Borio and Fritz (1994) 'The Response of Short Term Bank Lending Rates: a Cross-country Perspective' in *Financial Structure and the Monetary Transmission Mechanism*, Bank for International Settlements, March 1994.

Cotarelli, C. and Kourelis, A. (1994) 'Financial Structure, Bank Lending Rates and the Transmission Mechanism of Monetary Policy', IMF Working Paper, March 1994.

European Commission (1992) 'Report of the Committee of Independent Experts on Company Taxation', 1992.

European Commission (1996) 'A Common System of VAT', COM 328 (96), Brussels.

Frankel, J. and Rose, A. (1996) 'The Endogeneity of the Optimum Currency Area Criteria', CEPR Discussion Paper No. 1473, September.

Goodhart, C. (1995) 'The External Dimension of EMU', LSE Financial Markets Group Special Paper No. 42.

Miles, D. (1994) 'Fixed and Floating Rate Debt in the United Kingdom and Abroad', in *Bank of England Quarterly Bulletin*, February 1994.

Roll et al. (1993) 'Independent and Accountable: a New Mandate for the Bank of England', CEPR, October.

Roseveare, D., Leibfritz, W., Fore, D. and Wurzel E. (1996) 'Ageing Populations, Pension Systems and Government Budgets: Simulations for 20 OECD Countries', Economics Department Working Paper No. 168, OECD, Paris.

von Hagen, J. and Hammond, G. (1995) 'Regional Insurance Against Asymmetric Shocks. An Empirical Study for the European Community', CEPR Discussion Paper 1170, May.

Notes

1. They assume that demand shocks only have long-run impacts on prices, while supply shocks are those that can also affect output in the long run.

2. We assume here for simplicity that the deficit to GDP ratio is approximately normally distributed.

3. This is true if the tax rate paid on income earned on foreign assets is no higher than the domestic tax rate; in this case a double tax agreement means that extra domestic tax is paid to bring the tax rate into line with that levied on domestic assets. If tax on overseas asset income is levied at a higher rate domestic governments do not offer tax rebates. Note that residents of a high tax country could only take advantage of different tax rates by residing in a low tax country so the pressure to harmonize capital taxation depends on labour mobility.

4. If, however, the UK labour market were to adjust faster than continental European labour markets there is the possibility that after a shock monetary policy of the ECB would be kept tighter (or looser) for longer than is appropriate for UK conditions.

5. 'The External Dimension of EMU', LSE Financial Markets Group Special Paper No. 42, 1995.